FOOD ~~~ FIT FOR ~~~ PHARAOHS

FOOD FIT FOR PHARAOHS

AN ANCIENT EGYPTIAN COOKBOOK

MICHELLE BERRIEDALE-JOHNSON

THE BRITISH MUSEUM PRESS

The author and publishers are grateful for advice from Neal Spencer and Richard Parkinson, of the British Museum Department of Ancient Egypt and Sudan, and Neil Hewison, of The American University in Cairo Press

Michelle Berriedale-Johnson has asserted the right to be identified as the author of this work

First published in 1999 by The British Museum Press
A division of The British Museum Company Ltd
38 Russell Square, London WC1B 3QQ
www.britishmuseum.org

Reprinted 2005
First published in paperback 2008

A catalogue record for this book is available from the British Library

ISBN 978-0-7141-1984-7

Photography by the British Museum Department of Photography and Imaging
Line drawings by Kitty Chan
Designed and typeset in Bembo, Gill and Lithos by Harry Green
Cover design by Harry Green and Peter Ward
Printed in China by South China Printing Co. Ltd

CONTENTS

INTRODUCTION

The great River Nile – rising in the uplands of Africa, flowing through the deserts of Sudan and Nubia and finally down through the fertile plains of lower Egypt to the sea – has always been the life blood of the Egyptians. In the ancient world foreigners marvelled at the richness of Egypt's natural produce: fruit and vegetables, beans and pulses, grains, fish and wildfowl, birds and animals. All were available in abundance thanks to the yearly inundations which flooded the banks of the river, depositing rich layers of silt and irrigating the crops.

The Ancient Egyptians lived well. Although they left no recipe books, we can still get a good idea of what the pharaohs and their people may have eaten from the wall paintings in their tombs, the meals they buried with the dead to ensure that they did not go hungry in the next world, and from the tales of travellers such as the Greek Herodotus.

Bread was – and still is in much of North Africa – the staff of life. Early bakers used millet, barley and wheat for their flour. This had to be ground laboriously on a stone quern before being baked into flat and rather chewy loaves. The development of spelt, a new variety of wheat containing more gluten, allowed bakers to get a greater lift into the bread and to create the kind of flat pocket loaves (or pitta breads) that can be found all over North Africa today. (Spelt is now available once more in health-food stores, if you want to be truly authentic about your Egyptian cooking.) Bread was served with every meal and was used to scoop up the foods which could not be eaten by hand. Pieces of bread were also used, with the addition of yeast, to make the thick, rather gritty beer which was the common drink in Ancient Egypt. Bread was even used for paying wages, from the lowliest farm worker (who received just enough bread for his family) to important officials who might be 'paid' hundreds or thousands of loaves per day – which they in turn 'paid' to their subordinates.

Equally important to the average Ancient Egyptian was the daily dish of beans: brown fava beans, flat white or green broad beans and chick peas. The fava beans were cooked long and slowly, flavoured with garlic and lemon and eaten for breakfast, as a mid-morning snack, for lunch, tea and dinner. Broad beans were cooked into soups, added to stews and meat dishes, made into salads and served as mezze or hors d'oeuvre. Chick peas were puréed, added to stews or made into salads. No day's food would be complete without beans in some guise or other.

Other vital components of the diet were fresh vegetables and fruit. Great was the amazement of ancient travellers when they saw how many raw vegetables the Egyptians ate – onions, garlic, cucumbers, celery, radishes, olives and fresh herbs such as parsley and coriander. All were used both raw and cooked to accompany the beans and breads and to flavour soups and stews.

The generous waters of the Nile also allowed the inhabitants of its banks to grow luscious fruits, which the sun could then dry for long keeping. Fresh lemons and limes, possibly introduced by the Romans, were used as seasoning.

Dates, plums, figs, pomegranates, grapes, almonds, walnuts and pine nuts could be eaten fresh or used to make refreshing fruit compotes or rich and sweet pastries to nibble after the meal or as between-meal snacks. Grapes were also used to make red and white Egyptian wine. Both were widely respected in the ancient world, although only the palace officials and the rich could afford to drink them.

The Nile also supported a large population of fish and water fowl. In flood times fishermen did not even need to catch the fish, which would be left floundering on the banks as the floodwaters receded. Simply grilled and served with a tasty sauce, fresh Nile fish was a dish fit for a king – or pharaoh. Ducks, geese, herons and other waterfowl were also popular and could be roasted over an open fire or baked in a clay oven.

Sun and salt were used to dry and preserve fish for future use and to flavour them. One of the favourite dishes of many modern Egyptians is dried mullet roes (batarekh) — an acquired taste for foreigners but one for which expatriate Egyptians would sell their souls.

The fertile banks of the river also provided lush feeding for farm animals. Oxen were used for ploughing rather than for eating, but sheep, goats and pigs (known as 'small cattle') were popular with poorer families as they could be supported on relatively little ground. Sheep and goats also supplied milk and, therefore, cheese, while pigs acted as recycling centres for waste food which would otherwise have rotted in the hot climate. Chicken were good 'recyclers' too — and they laid eggs. (Disposing of rotting food was an ongoing problem for Ancient Egyptian villages. All too often it would just be thrown into the street or the river. The former encouraged the ever-present vermin, the latter polluted the water.)

Ancient Egyptian houses — and therefore cooking facilities — were simple. The main building materials were mud bricks (easily available and easy to use). Although the inside walls of the houses were often brightly painted, the houses were cramped and used mainly for sleeping. Food was often cooked out of doors on an open fire. Alternatively a kitchen room was built at the back of the house, or even separate from it so as to reduce the risk of fire. Small bread ovens often had flat tops which also provided heat for slow-cooking soups and stews.

Because the quality of their raw materials was so good, Egyptian cooks had little need for complex recipes to disguise poor ingredients — unlike fellow cooks in less fertile parts of the ancient world. Recipes, therefore, remained simple: roasting and grilling for meats and fish, long slow cooking with just a few vegetables or herbs for beans and pulses. No preparation at all was needed for salad vegetables, herbs or fruit, which were rarely cooked.

In fact, as anyone who travels through modern Egypt will realize, not much has changed — apart from the introduction of potatoes, aubergines and tomatoes from South America. This means that, although we have no authentic recipes to follow (like those of Apicius, the Roman gastronome, or Carême, the great French master chef), it is still possible to create dishes that will not taste very different from those eaten by the workmen who laboured to construct the great pyramids of the pharaohs.

The food of Ancient Egypt, once cooked, was very simple to eat. Forks were unknown, and the flat loaves of bread were used as containers and 'spoons'. It was quite acceptable to use your fingers to eat meat and fish – indeed, some tomb paintings show rich ladies holding whole birds in their hands, ready for a good chew. Soup would be drunk out of bowls, and vegetables, fruit and desserts eaten with the fingers.

Dishes were set out on a low table; diners sat around on low stools and helped themselves to whatever they wanted. Alternatively the food would be laid on rush mats on the ground and the diners would sit around the mats. Wines and beers were drunk copiously with meals and apparently it was no disgrace to get drunk. Some tomb paintings show quite grand ladies being unselfconsciously sick during the course of a lengthy banquet!

If you wish to create an Egyptian meal for yourself (with or without the excess of wine), you should have little difficulty in locating most of the ingredients used in the recipes which follow. Middle Eastern grocery shops can now be found in most large cities, and even if you cannot get fresh ingredients (such as molokhia leaves), you can usually find them dried. Where you might have problems I have suggested an alternative.

If you are inspired to explore the cooking of Ancient (and modern) Egypt further, you could do no better than to read the works of Claudia Roden (to whom I am grateful for her permission to use her recipes for cousbareia sauce, glazed walnuts and dried fig and apricot jam) and Suzy Benghiat (thanks to her for the use of her recipe for chicken kishk). You will find details of their books and others you might want to look at in the list of Further Reading. Alternatively you could go to Egypt to sample in real life the foods which so impressed not only the well-heeled ancient traveller Herodotus, but even the 'Children of Israel' on their long trek home through the desert, freed at last from their many years of slavery in Egypt:

Will no one give us meat? In Egypt we had fish for the asking, cucumbers and watermelons, leeks and onions and garlic. Now our throats are parched; there is nothing wherever we look except this manna.

SOUPS, STARTERS AND SNACKS

As in most ancient cultures, soups made from vegetables and pulses, flavoured with herbs and enriched with meat or fish when available, formed the staple food of working families. In Egypt the passion for beans of all kinds still inspires soup making, and soups are often served as a meal on their own accompanied only by Egyptian flat or pitta bread. Most soups use the traditional flavourings of garlic, lemon, parsley, cumin and coriander, so feel free to adjust the quantities of these to suit your own taste.

Mezze or hors d'oeuvres have always been popular in Egypt both as a meal on their own or as the starting course for a more substantial lunch or dinner: endless little dishes of bean pastes, salads, herbs, eggs, meat and fish stews, into which you dip pieces of the Egyptian flat bread which is, in itself, as old as the pharaohs' tombs. All of these dishes can be used as part of a mezze, but they can also be served on their own as starters or snacks. If you wanted to add more choices to your mezze table, you could include small dishes of eggah, vegetarian foods and tagins from the next section.

MOLOKHIA

Molokhia is one of the most ancient of Egyptian dishes, believed to be portrayed in pharaonic tomb paintings, and has been the staple food of the Egyptian peasant from time immemorial. Each family has its own recipe for molokhia, whether served as a soup or as a richer main dish filled with meats and other vegetables as it was in the Middle Ages. The fresh leaves (which look a bit like spinach) are seldom available outside Egypt, but dried molokhia leaves can usually be found in Greek and Middle Eastern shops. If you wish to serve it as a main course rather than a soup, triple the quantity of meat and accompany with rice cooked in the stock.

SERVES 6

350 g/12 oz lamb, chicken or duck

2 onions, finely chopped

9 garlic cloves, crushed

sea salt and freshly ground black pepper

75 g/3 oz dried molokhia leaves

2 tbsp clarified butter or olive oil

2 tbsp ground coriander

½ tsp chilli or cayenne pepper

3 extra onions, thinly sliced with 2 tbsp vinegar to garnish (optional)

Put the meat with the chopped onions, a third of the crushed garlic and a generous seasoning of salt and pepper into a large pan and pour in 1.75 litres/3 pints/7½ cups of fresh water. Bring slowly to the boil, skimming any scum which may rise to the surface, and simmer for 2 hours. Remove the meat from the stock, discard any bones and chop it into reasonably small pieces. Strain the stock into a large clean pan.

If you wish to serve the dish with rice as an accompaniment, cook 175 g/6 oz patna or basmati rice in 600 ml/1 pint/2½ cups of the stock. Add a little more stock if the rice seems too dry; if there is too much liquid, simply drain it off and return it to the stock pot.

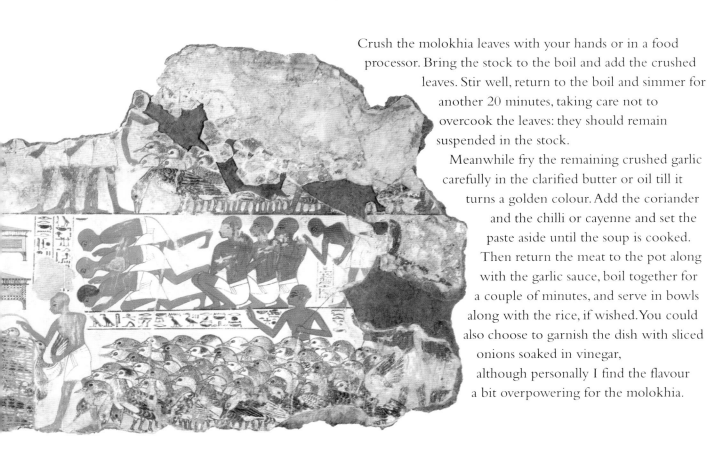

Crush the molokhia leaves with your hands or in a food processor. Bring the stock to the boil and add the crushed leaves. Stir well, return to the boil and simmer for another 20 minutes, taking care not to overcook the leaves: they should remain suspended in the stock.

Meanwhile fry the remaining crushed garlic carefully in the clarified butter or oil till it turns a golden colour. Add the coriander and the chilli or cayenne and set the paste aside until the soup is cooked. Then return the meat to the pot along with the garlic sauce, boil together for a couple of minutes, and serve in bowls along with the rice, if wished. You could also choose to garnish the dish with sliced onions soaked in vinegar, although personally I find the flavour a bit overpowering for the molokhia.

BROAD BEAN SOUP

SERVES 6

350 g/12 oz dried skinned broad beans

2 tbsp olive oil

juice of 1 small lemon

sea salt and freshly ground black pepper

finely chopped fresh parsley

This is the simplest of bean soups but is extraordinarily delicious. Because it is both nutritious and easy to digest, it is often served to convalescents to help rebuild their strength. It should be made from white skinned broad beans, which ought to be available from Greek or Middle Eastern grocers. If you can only find them with their skins on, they will need extra soaking to make the skins easier to remove. If you cannot find any kind of dried broad bean, you could substitute dried butter beans or white haricot beans.

Soak the beans in plenty of cold water overnight. Next day, discard the soaking water, rinse the beans and put them in a deep pan with 1.5 litres/ 2½ pints/6 cups fresh cold water. Bring to the boil and simmer gently for 2–3 hours or till the beans are very soft. Purée the mixture in a food processor (or press through a sieve), then return it to the pan. Add the oil and lemon juice, and salt and pepper to taste. Serve sprinkled with lots of freshly chopped parsley.

ROASTED CHICK PEAS WITH NUTS AND SEEDS

This is a delicious snack to add to the mezze table, but the mixture is also excellent to serve with drinks – or to take on a hike, as a sort of Egyptian trail mix!

200 g/7 oz cooked dried (see p. 20) or drained canned chick peas (garbanzos)

200 g/7 oz mixed nuts (almonds, walnuts, pine nuts, etc.) and seeds (pumpkin, sunflower, etc.)

juice of 2 lemons

sea salt and freshly ground black pepper

Put the chick peas with the nuts and seeds in a small pan. Add the lemon juice and just enough water to cover them, plus a generous shake of salt and pepper. Bring to the boil and simmer for 5–6 minutes, then drain.

Spread the mixture out on a flat ovenproof tray or dish and bake for 20–25 minutes in a preheated moderate oven (180°C/350°F/Gas Mark 4), shaking it every now and then to mix the peas, nuts and seeds around and checking to make sure that they do not burn.

Serve at once or store in an airtight container for up to two weeks.

SHOURBAT ADS

Lentils of any colour can be used for this soup, although the red ones look the most attractive and disintegrate fastest. It is delicious on its own or served with garlic croûtons or garlic sauce.

SERVES 6

2 tbsp olive oil

1 large onion, chopped

2 large garlic cloves, sliced

1 large celery stick, chopped

2 tsp ground cumin

1 tsp ground coriander

375 g/13 oz red lentils

2 litres/3½ pints/9 cups chicken or vegetable stock, or water

sea salt and freshly ground black pepper

Put the oil in a deep pan with the onion, garlic and celery and cook gently for 5–10 minutes or until the vegetables are starting to soften. Add the spices and the lentils and continue to cook for a few minutes more, then add the liquid and a little seasoning. Bring to the boil and simmer gently for 45–60 minutes or till the lentils have all but disintegrated. Purée them in a food processor then return to the pan, reheat and adjust the seasoning to taste. Serve the soup alone with plenty of bread or complemented by the addition of garlic croûtons or garlic sauce (opposite).

GARLIC CROÛTONS

8–10 tbsp olive oil

3 garlic cloves, crushed

3 slices brown bread, cut into small cubes

Heat the oil in a wide frying pan. Add the garlic and cook gently for several minutes or till it is lightly cooked through. Increase the heat and add the bread cubes. Fry briskly for 5–6 minutes till the cubes are all well-browned but not burnt. Remove from the pan and drain on kitchen paper. Serve warm.

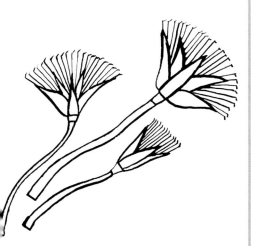

GARLIC SAUCE

2 tbsp olive oil or clarified butter

3–4 garlic cloves, crushed

½ tsp ground coriander

½ tsp ground cumin

Heat the oil or butter and briskly fry the garlic with the spices until it is golden brown but not burnt. Add sizzling hot, in small spoonfuls, to each serving.

HUMMUS

Chick peas are a great favourite with Egyptian cooks, and this simple, garlic-flavoured purée is the most popular way of serving them. You can vary the amounts of garlic and lemon juice to suit your own taste.

SERVES 4–6 AS A DIP OR PÂTÉ

250 g/9 oz dried chick peas (garbanzos) or 1 × 400-g/14-oz can

1–2 garlic cloves, sliced

large pinch of ground cumin

juice of 1 lemon

2 tbsp olive oil

sea salt and freshly ground black pepper

If you have time, you can soak dried chick peas for the hummus; if you are in a hurry, substitute canned. For dried chick peas, soak overnight in water to cover, drain and then simmer them for 1–2 hours in fresh water. Salt them lightly, cook for another 15 minutes, then drain, reserving a little of the cooking water. If you are using canned chick peas, drain them and reserve a little of the liquid from the can.

Put the chick peas into a food processor or a mouli legumes with 2 tbsp of their cooking water or liquid from the can. Add the garlic, cumin, lemon juice and oil, and purée. Add salt and pepper to taste and a little more liquid if the purée is too thick. Serve with fresh warm pitta bread and raw vegetables.

HUMMUS BI TAHINA

Adding tahini (sesame seed paste) to hummus is so common that the combination is often just called 'hummus'. You can use a medium or dark paste, depending on how strong a tahini flavour you like. You will find tahini paste in most good delicatessens as well as Greek and Middle Eastern shops.

250 g/9 oz dried chick peas (garbanzos) or 1 × 400-g/14-oz can

juice of 1 lemon

2 garlic cloves, sliced

pinch of cayenne pepper

2 tbsp tahini (sesame seed paste)

sea salt

1 tbsp olive oil

pinch of paprika

a little chopped fresh parsley

For dried chick peas, soak and cook them as described opposite, reserving a little of the cooking water. If using canned chick peas, drain, reserving a little of their liquid.

Put the chick peas into a food processor or mouli legumes with 2 tbsp of their cooking water or liquid from the can. Add the lemon juice, garlic, cayenne and tahini and purée to a smooth, soft cream. Season to taste with salt, then pour into a flattish bowl. When ready to serve, dribble the olive oil over the top and sprinkle with a little paprika and chopped parsley. Serve with fresh warm pitta bread and raw vegetables.

BABA GHANOUJ

Aubergines (eggplant) are very popular all over North Africa, and variations on this rich pâté or dip are legion. Adapting the spices and seasonings in this recipe to suit your own taste is thus in the best Egyptian tradition.

SERVES 6 AS A DIP OR PÂTÉ

2 large aubergines (eggplant)

2 garlic cloves

2 tbsp tahini (sesame seed paste)

juice of 1 lemon

½ tsp ground cumin

½ pitta bread, broken into pieces

sea salt and freshly ground black pepper

chopped fresh parsley

Cook the aubergines under a hot grill (or over charcoal, if you can manage it) till the skin on each side blackens and blisters and the flesh inside is very soft. Allow to cool, then peel off the skin and squeeze any excess water from the flesh.

Put the flesh of the aubergine into a food processor along with the garlic, tahini, lemon juice, cumin and pitta bread, and purée. Season to taste and sprinkle with plenty of chopped parsley. Serve with fresh warm pitta bread.

OLIVE SALAD

Olives are among the most ancient trees found in Europe – not quite dating back to the pharaohs' tombs, although some are said to live to be over 1,000 years old. Prepare this salad 24 hours before you want to use it, to allow the flavours to amalgamate.

SERVES 6–8

scant tsp sea salt

3 garlic cloves, crushed

pinch of chilli powder

½ tsp paprika

1 tsp ground cumin

juice of 3 lemons

6 tbsp olive oil

400 g/14 oz pitted mixed green and black olives

4 tbsp chopped fresh parsley

Mix all but the last two ingredients well together to make the dressing, then add the olives and parsley and combine thoroughly. Cover and leave for several hours or overnight to marinate before serving as part of a mezze or as a side salad.

AUBERGINE SALAD

If you double the quantities, you could serve this salad as a vegetarian main course for a summer lunch. It is surprisingly rich and filling.

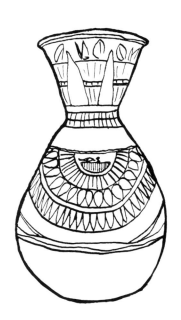

SERVES 4

2 large aubergines (eggplant)

sea salt and freshly ground black pepper

8 tbsp olive oil

2 green peppers, seeded and thinly sliced

2 onions, sliced

2 garlic cloves, finely sliced

1 tsp coriander seeds, lightly crushed

juice of 1 lemon

large handful fresh coriander leaves, chopped

Thinly slice the aubergines, lay them out in a colander and sprinkle with salt. Leave to sweat for at least 30 minutes, then rinse and dry the slices.

Heat the oil in a wide, heavy pan and place the aubergine slices in it, in a single layer. Fry briskly till they are browned on one side. Turn the slices over and add the green peppers, onions, garlic and coriander seeds. Reduce the heat and continue to fry very gently for 10–15 minutes or till the onions and aubergines are well tanned and cooked through.

Turn the vegetables into a serving dish and sprinkle with salt, pepper and lemon juice. Just before serving, sprinkle generously with the chopped fresh coriander leaves.

COURGETTE AND CHICK PEA SALAD

You can also serve this salad warm as a vegetable accompaniment to a meat dish.

SERVES 6

4 tbsp olive oil

3 garlic cloves, sliced

2 onions, sliced

4 large courgettes (zucchini), sliced into rounds

½ tsp cayenne pepper

1 × 400-g/14-oz can chick peas (garbanzos), drained

50 g/2 oz black olives, pitted and halved

juice of 2 lemons

sea salt and freshly ground black pepper

2 handfuls fresh parsley, chopped

Heat the oil in a wide, heavy pan and sweat the garlic and onions for a few minutes. Add the courgettes, cayenne pepper and chick peas. Cover and simmer for 5 minutes, then remove the lid and continue to cook for a further 5 minutes or till the courgettes are quite soft.

Add the olives, lemon juice, and salt and pepper to taste. Stir in the chopped parsley just before serving.

TA'AMIA

Ta'amia (also known as tameya) are broad bean rissoles, one of the most traditional of Egyptian dishes and a favourite with the Christian Copts, who are said to be the purest descendants of the Ancient Egyptians. The rissoles should be made with dried broad beans, which are very popular in southern Europe and can usually be found in Middle Eastern food shops. However, if you have difficulty locating them, the ta'amia are still excellent made with dried butter beans. Formed into small round balls rather than the traditional patties, they make perfect cocktail snacks.

SERVES 6

450 g/1 lb dried broad beans
2 large onions, chopped
4 large garlic cloves
1 tbsp ground coriander
2 tsp ground cumin
½ teaspoon baking powder or soda
generous shake of Tabasco sauce
1 tsp sea salt
freshly ground black pepper
sesame or poppy seeds for coating (optional)
oil for deep-frying

Soak the beans for 24 hours, then pop them out of their skins and put them in a food processor with the onions, garlic, coriander, cumin, baking powder, Tabasco, salt and plenty of pepper. Process very thoroughly till you have

a smooth paste; if it is not smooth, the patties will disintegrate in the cooking. If you do not have a processor, use a liquidizer, or pound the mixture by hand in a pestle and mortar – hard work, but that is how it would originally have been done. Set the purée aside for at least 30 minutes, then form it into flat round cakes 3–4 cm (1–1½ in) across. Coat them in sesame or poppy seeds – this is not essential, but it makes the ta'amia even more delicious. Set them aside for a further 15 minutes.

Heat the oil till a piece of bread dropped in it is well tanned in 1 minute. Gently lower the rissoles down into the oil and deep-fry for 2–3 minutes or till they are nicely browned all over. Remove from the oil, drain on kitchen paper and serve accompanied by fresh salads and breads.

BEID HAMINE

These are eggs which have been cooked very long and slowly so that they are meltingly soft and creamy in the middle. They are used as a garnish for soups and stews but are most popular served with ful medames (opposite).

SERVES 6

6 eggs

skins from several large onions, or 1 tbsp ground coffee

Put the eggs with either the onion skins or the ground coffee (I think onion skins give a better flavour) in a large pan, cover well with water and cook on the lowest possible heat, or in a slow cooker, for at least 6 hours. Alternatively, if you are cooking ful medames, put the eggs (well scrubbed) and onion skins in with the beans to cook. Remove and shell the eggs (remember to remove the onion skins as well if you are cooking them in a pot of ful) and serve with the ful medames or in a stew or casserole.

FUL MEDAMES

Ful medames (pronounced 'fool medamess'), slowly cooked brown fava beans, is the national dish of Egypt and probably dates back to the pharaohs. The beans are eaten by rich and poor, for breakfast, lunch and dinner, with bread, lentils, sauces, salads and, most frequently, eggs. Traditionally the beans are cooked in an *idra*, a special earthenware pot tapering at the neck to reduce evaporation of the cooking water to a minimum, but any heavy pot with a well-fitting lid will do. Seasoning (apart from the addition of some garlic once the beans are cooked) is done at the table.

SERVES 6

450 g/1 lb dried ful (brown fava beans)

2–4 garlic cloves, crushed

chopped fresh parsley

Dried fava beans are obtainable from most Greek and Middle Eastern shops. You can also buy them tinned, in which case you would not need to soak or cook them first but simply warm before stirring in the garlic. If you cannot find brown fava beans, another variety of dried broad beans could be substituted.

Rinse the dried beans and soak them in water to cover for a minimum of 8 hours. Then put them in a large saucepan, well-covered with fresh water, bring to the boil, cover the pan and simmer until they are tender but not mushy. This can take anything from 2 to 6 hours, depending on how dry the beans were; you could also use a slow cooker to cook the beans overnight, or cook them in a pressure cooker which reduces the cooking time to 30–45 minutes; a microwave will not reduce the cooking time. Once the beans are cooked, drain them and stir in the crushed garlic.

Serve the beans warm, in bowls, sprinkled with chopped parsley, accompanied with oil or butter and lemon juice, salt, pepper, cumin and cayenne pepper, or topped with hamine eggs (opposite).

MAIN DISHES

Egyptian main courses could almost be described as 'grown-up' mezze. Meat stews or tagins, offered as part of the mezze table, are simply served in larger portions as main dishes. The much-loved beans reappear in stews and vegetable dishes, flavoured as usual with lemon and coriander. Main dishes are normally accompanied by a salad of raw vegetables dressed with oil and lemon juice.

On special occasions whole fish or birds will be cooked and served on the bone. Chicken and pigeon are the most popular, although duck is not uncommon. Generally stuffed with herbs, spices and grains of some kind, they are then elaborately decorated with lemon slices, pickles and nuts.

LEEK, COURGETTE AND PINE NUT EGGAH

SERVES 6

2 tbsp butter

3 large leeks, finely sliced

2 large courgettes (zucchini), finely sliced

1 pitta bread, broken into pieces and soaked in 6 tbsp milk

2 tbsp pine nuts or flaked almonds

8 eggs

sea salt and freshly ground black pepper

As many tomb paintings show, birds and fowl have always been a feature of Egyptian life and therefore Egyptian cooking. Although the birds themselves are popular in main dishes, eggs are also widely used, especially in the rich eggah, or omelet, which is much closer to a Spanish tortilla than to a conventional French omelette. An eggah can be filled with vegetables, herbs, nuts and spices and can include meat or fish, so feel free to experiment with fillings. It can be cooked in the oven or on a hob, and because it is so much more solid than an ordinary omelette, it is also more versatile. Eggahs are just as good cold as hot.

Heat the butter in a wide, deep, heavy frying pan and add the leeks and courgettes. Cover and cook very gently till they are quite soft. Mix in the pitta bread pieces and the pine nuts. Beat the eggs in a bowl, season with salt and pepper and add them to the vegetables, stirring well. Cover the pan and cook slowly for 10–15 minutes or until the eggah is cooked through. Remove carefully from the pan and serve warm or set aside to cool. Cut the eggah into wedges. These can be served as part of a mezze or with drinks and are excellent for picnics or box lunches.

RICE WITH BROAD BEANS AND CORIANDER

This is a delicious vegetarian salad which combines two Egyptian favourites, broad beans and rice, plus all the classic flavourings. It can be served on its own, as a side vegetable with a meat or fish tagin, or as part of a mezze table.

SERVES 6

4 tbsp olive oil

2 large celery sticks, finely chopped

1 large onion, finely chopped

2 garlic cloves, finely sliced

1 tsp lightly crushed coriander seeds

6 tbsp long-grain rice

sea salt and freshly ground black pepper

400 g/14 oz fresh or frozen broad beans

50 g/2 oz pine nuts

juice of ½ lemon

2 large handfuls of fresh coriander, chopped

Heat the oil in a wide, heavy pan and add the celery, onion and garlic. Cook gently for 8–10 minutes or until the onion is translucent. Add the coriander seeds, rice and a little seasoning and continue to cook gently for another 3–4 minutes, then add 800 ml/1½ pints/3½ cups water. Bring to the boil and cook briskly for 10–15 minutes or until most of the water is absorbed and the rice is cooked (both time and amount of liquid will vary, according to the type of rice).

Add the beans and pine nuts and continue to cook for a further 5–8 minutes to allow the flavours to amalgamate. Add the lemon juice and fresh coriander and adjust the seasoning to taste. Serve warm or at room temperature.

SPINACH WITH RICE AND PINE NUTS

This is a delicious combination of classic Egyptian ingredients in which the rice plays a very happy second fiddle to the spinach. As usual, it can be served as a dish on its own, as an accompaniment to a meat or fish dish or as part of a mezze table.

SERVES 6

6 tbsp olive oil

2 large garlic cloves, finely sliced

large pinch of chilli powder

500 g/1½ lb fresh spinach, washed and dried

6 tbsp long-grain rice

juice of 1½–2 lemons

sea salt and freshly ground black pepper

2 tbsp pine nuts

Heat the oil in a wide, heavy pan and add the garlic, chilli powder, a large pinch of salt and the spinach. Cook quickly for a few minutes till the spinach wilts. Add the rice and 800 ml/1½ pints/3½ cups water, bring to the boil and simmer briskly, covered, for 20–30 minutes or till the rice is cooked. Add the juice of 1½–2 lemons (depending on size), black pepper to taste and the pine nuts. Serve warm or at room temperature.

CAULIFLOWER WITH ANCHOVIES AND LEMON

Both potatoes and cauliflower are post-pharaonic arrivals in Egyptian cuisine but are now widely used. In Egypt this dish would probably be made with the much-loved batarekh (dried mullet roe), but this is difficult to find outside Egypt so anchovies make a very successful substitute.

SERVES 4

4 medium potatoes, halved

1 medium cauliflower, broken into florets

3 tbsp olive oil

6 canned anchovy fillets plus 2 tbsp oil from the can

2 garlic cloves, crushed

juice of 2 lemons

sea salt and freshly ground black pepper

Steam the potatoes for 15–20 minutes till just cooked, then cut into large dice. Meanwhile, steam the cauliflower in a separate pan for 10–15 minutes, till just cooked but still slightly crunchy.

Heat the oil in a wide, heavy pan and add the anchovies, 2 tbsp of their oil and the garlic. Cook for several minutes till the anchovies have partially dissolved. Add the lemon juice and a little salt and pepper, then add the potatoes and cauliflower. Toss well in the sauce and leave to marinate for at least 30 minutes before serving warm or at room temperature.

EGYPTIAN FISH WITH COUSBAREIA SAUCE

Frying fish, whole or in slices, is both a popular and traditional way of serving fish in Egypt. Red mullet is a favourite and delicious, but expensive; you could substitute any firm-fleshed white fish in this recipe. Generally fried fish needs only lemon wedges to set it off, though a wide variety of local sauces are served. In this one the hazelnuts give an interesting texture and the pine nuts a wonderful flavour.

SERVES 6

about 1 kg/2½ lb white fish

flour for coating

clean oil for deep-frying

2 tbsp olive oil

2 onions, thinly sliced

115 g/4 oz hazelnuts, coarsely chopped

50 g/2 oz pine nuts

225 g/8 oz tomatoes, sliced

3 tbsp finely chopped fresh parsley

sea salt and freshly ground black pepper

Clean the fish carefully, cutting larger fish into thick slices and leaving smaller ones whole. Dry the pieces very thoroughly, then dredge with flour. Meanwhile, heat the oil for deep-frying till it is very hot and then gently lower the fish pieces into it. Do not try to cook too many at the same time, as the temperature of the oil must remain as hot as possible or the fish will go soggy. After 5–10 minutes the fish should be crisp and a light golden colour. Remove the pieces from the oil and drain on kitchen paper. They can be served as they are with salt, pepper and lemon wedges if you prefer, otherwise continue as below.

Heat the olive oil in a deep pan and fry the onions

till they are soft and just turning golden. Add the hazelnuts and pine nuts and fry for a couple of minutes more, then add the tomato slices and cook till they soften. Add just enough water to cover the vegetables, stir in the parsley, season to taste with salt and pepper and simmer for another few minutes. Carefully lay the fish pieces in the pan and spoon a little of the sauce over them. Cover the pan and simmer gently for 15 minutes. Alternatively, place the fish pieces in an ovenproof dish, pour the sauce over and cook in a preheated moderate oven (180°C/350°F/Gas Mark 4) for 15 minutes. Serve warm with rice or new potatoes.

FISH WITH TARATOR SAUCE

A large whole fish – baked or barbecued and ornately decorated with lemon slices, pine nuts, pickles, olives and radishes, all arranged in a complex oriental design – often forms the centrepiece of a grand Middle Eastern dinner. The fish will be accompanied by bowls of tarator sauce which, according to taste and whether you are in Egypt, Iran or Turkey, can be based on pine nuts, almonds or hazelnuts. The sauce is also delicious served as a dressing for almost any vegetable, hot or cold. For this recipe choose a very fresh whole firm-fleshed fish, large enough to serve six, and do not discard the head or tail.

SERVES 6

1 whole firm-fleshed white fish, cleaned
sea salt and freshly ground black pepper
olive oil
2 lemons
115 g/4 oz pine nuts, almonds or hazelnuts
1 thick slice white bread, crust removed
1–2 large garlic cloves

Rub the fish well with salt, pepper and olive oil, making a few slits in its skin with a sharp knife so that the seasoning goes right through. Slice one of the lemons. Wrap the fish in foil dotted with the lemon slices and bake in a preheated moderate oven (180°C/350°F/Gas Mark 4) for about 10 minutes per 450 g/1 lb, or until the skin lifts easily off the flesh. Remove the fish carefully, reserving the juices. Skin and fillet it, keeping the head and tail, and arrange the fillets on a serving dish. Replace the head and tail at the top and bottom and decorate the fish as ornately as you like with more lemon slices, toasted pine nuts or almond slivers, sliced olives, sliced pimiento, sprigs of fresh coriander, etc.

To make the sauce, skin the nuts if they are not already skinned (almond skins will pop off easily if soaked for 5 minutes in boiling water, whereas hazelnuts are best toasted in a low oven until the skins are brittle, when they can be rubbed off). Then put them into a food processor or liquidizer with the bread, garlic, ½ tsp salt, the juice from the remaining lemon, the reserved fish cooking juices and 150 ml/5 fl oz/⅔ cup water. Blend until you have a fairly smooth sauce, adding a little more water if the sauce is too thick: it should be the consistency of a thick coating. Adjust the seasoning to taste and serve the sauce in bowls with the fish.

TAGINS

Although the word has now come to designate the stew that is cooked in it, a tagin is in fact an earthenware stewing pot with a narrow neck, widely used all over North Africa. It has the virtue of reducing evaporation while allowing the dish to cook slowly for a very long time, using a minimum of heat. The long slow cooking allows the use of cheap (probably tough) cuts of meat and gets the most flavour from the spices and herbs. To get closest to tagin cooking in a modern kitchen you need a slow cooker or a heavy pan with a well-fitting lid and a long slow cooking time.

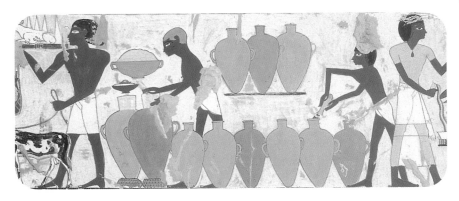

Lamb or mutton are the traditional meats throughout North Africa, including Egypt. Although oxen were once used the length of the Nile for cultivation, they were rarely eaten. However, beef and veal have both become increasingly popular over the last century, though recipes have changed little, merely substituting beef for mutton and veal for lamb. You can use either.

BEEF OR LAMB TAGIN WITH CHICK PEAS AND CUMIN

4 tbsp olive oil

2 large or 4 medium onions, chopped

4 garlic cloves, crushed

600 g/1½ lb stewing beef or lamb, trimmed and cut into large pieces

2 tsp cumin seeds

300 g/12 oz dried chick peas (garbanzos), soaked in water overnight

400 g/14 oz new potatoes, scrubbed and cut in half or quartered

sea salt and freshly ground black pepper

3 handfuls fresh parsley or coriander, chopped

Heat the oil in a heavy pan just big enough to hold the meat and vegetables. Add the onions, garlic and meat and cook briskly until the meat is browned. Drain the chick peas and add to the pan with the potatoes, a little salt and pepper and enough water to just cover the meat and vegetables. Bring slowly to the boil, then cook *very* slowly (a slow cooker would be ideal) for 4–6 hours. The meat should be falling apart by the time the tagin is cooked. Adjust the seasoning to taste, sprinkle with plenty of chopped parsley or coriander and serve with salad and bread.

TAGIN OF BEEF OR LAMB WITH OKRA

f you cannot get fresh okra for this dish, you can substitute canned or bottled. It is easy to peel the skin off fresh tomatoes if you scald them first in boiling water for 3–4 minutes. This type of stew is ideal served with couscous, or alternatively with rice and bread.

SERVES 6

6 tbsp olive oil

3 onions, finely sliced

3 garlic cloves, finely sliced

200 g/7 oz fresh okra, topped and tailed and halved if large, or 150 g/5 oz canned or bottled okra

600 g/1½ lb stewing or braising beef or lamb, trimmed and diced

3 tsp tomato purée or paste

1 tsp ground cumin

6 tomatoes, skinned and diced

sea salt and freshly ground black pepper

Heat the oil in a heavy pan and add the onions, garlic and fresh okra. Cook together briskly for 3–4 minutes. Add the meat, tomato purée, cumin, chopped canned okra (if using) and diced tomatoes and continue to cook briskly for another 3–4 minutes. Add 300 ml/½ pint/1½ cups water and a little salt and pepper. Bring back to the boil, then turn the heat down very low and simmer very gently for 1½–2 hours, or until the meat is very tender. Adjust the seasoning to taste and serve with couscous or rice and a green salad.

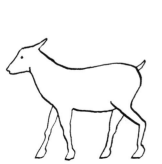

LAMB AND ARTICHOKE TAGIN

SERVES 4

3 tbsp olive oil

½ tsp sea salt

2 tsp ground turmeric

1 tsp ground ginger

3 garlic cloves, crushed

500 g/1½ lb fillet or shoulder of lamb, trimmed and diced

8 cooked fresh or drained canned artichoke hearts

juice of ½–1 lemon

Heat the oil in a deep heavy pan and add the spices and garlic. Fry briskly for a couple of minutes, taking care not to burn the paste, then add the meat and continue to fry briskly until it is well tanned all over. Add just enough water to cover the meat, bring back to the boil, cover the pan and simmer *very* gently for 2 hours or until the lamb is very tender.

Add the artichoke hearts and lemon juice and continue to cook for a further 10–15 minutes to amalgamate the flavours. Adjust the seasoning to taste and serve with plenty of rice or flat pitta bread.

FERIQUE CHICKEN

Recipes for meats cooked with whole wheat are to be found in medieval Arab cookery books and no doubt date back much earlier. If you cannot get whole wheat kernels you can use burghul (bulgar or cracked wheat), but it will cook more quickly and so may be slightly 'mushier' in texture. If you prefer you can use veal instead of chicken. The turmeric gives the whole dish a lovely golden colour. Like so many Middle Eastern dishes, this recipe requires long slow cooking to tenderize the ingredients and bring out their flavours. A slow cooker which can be left to simmer all night is ideal. Any liquid left over afterwards makes a delicious soup.

SERVES 6

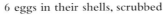

2 tbsp olive or sunflower oil

1 large onion, finely chopped

1 large chicken or 1 kg/2 lb knuckle of veal

1 calf's foot (if available), blanched

marrow bone pieces (if available)

6 eggs in their shells, scrubbed

225 g/8 oz whole wheat kernels, washed and soaked for up to 1 hour

1–2 tsp turmeric

sea salt and freshly ground black pepper

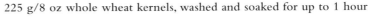

Heat the oil in a heavy pan just big enough to hold all the ingredients, or in a slow cooker. Add the onion and soften slightly, then add the meats, eggs, whole wheat and turmeric. Add enough water to cover fairly generously, cover the pan tightly and cook very gently over a low heat for 3–4 hours, or overnight in a slow cooker. The meat should be very tender, falling off the bones, and the wheat kernels swollen and well cooked. Remove the meat and bones from the pan, carve the meat and discard the bones. Shell the eggs and season the juices to taste. Serve the ferique – pieces of chicken or veal, eggs, wheat and juices – in deep bowls.

HAMAM MAHSHI

Stuffed pigeon is a celebration dish all over North Africa, but as they can be both tough and strong-flavoured you may prefer to use baby chickens or poussins. In either case, long slow cooking should ensure a tender bird.

SERVES 4

3 tbsp butter

1 medium onion, finely chopped

2 tbsp chicken livers, trimmed and finely chopped

4 tbsp burghul (cracked wheat)

1 tbsp chopped fresh parsley

1 tsp dried mint

600 ml/1 pint/2½ cups chicken or vegetable stock

sea salt and freshly ground black pepper

4 pigeons or poussins

Melt 1 tbsp of the butter in a large pan and gently cook the onion and chicken livers until the onion is soft. Add the burghul, parsley, mint and half the stock. Bring back to the boil and simmer gently for 10–15 minutes or until the wheat is soft and the liquid absorbed. Season to taste with salt and pepper.

Stuff the birds with the mixture, which should just fill 4 birds. Place them in a heavy casserole, just big enough to hold them, dot with the remaining butter and pour in the remaining stock. Cover the casserole and bake in a preheated oven at 160°C/325°F/Gas Mark 3 for 1½–2 hours or until the birds are really tender. Serve with the pan juices, bread and salad vegetables.

CHICKEN KISHK

Fowl of all kinds have always been popular with Egyptian cooks. Birds are often brought live to market or the poultry shop where they are killed and plucked. Claudia Roden tells of peasants and shopkeepers thrusting a large handful of corn down a bird's throat before killing it so as to increase the weight!

This rich and tasty chicken dish is a great favourite in Egypt, although the original kishk were in fact made from wheat boiled in soured milk, then dried in the sun: while still damp it could be formed into small balls or sticks and then chewed as sweets or used to thicken soups and stews.

SERVES 4

1 medium free-range chicken

4 onions, chopped

1 celery stick, chopped

2 sprigs fresh parsley

5–6 cardamom pods, cracked

sea salt and 6 black peppercorns

2 tbsp arrowroot

4 tbsp natural yoghurt

juice of ½ lemon

1 tbsp butter

2 tbsp oil

2 garlic cloves, finely sliced

Put the chicken in a large pan with one of the onions, the celery, parsley, cardamom, salt and peppercorns. Cover with water, bring slowly to the boil and simmer for 1–1½ hours or until the chicken is really tender. Remove the bird carefully from the pan. Discard the skin, remove the meat from the bones and set it aside. Return the carcass to the pan and continue to simmer the bones for another hour. Leave to cool slightly, then strain the stock and discard the bones.

Mix the arrowroot with the yoghurt and lemon juice in a bowl, then gradually add 5–6 ladlefuls of chicken stock. Pour into a small saucepan and cook over a gentle

heat for 10–15 minutes or until the sauce has thickened considerably. Season to taste.

Meanwhile, heat the butter with the oil and gently fry the remaining onions with the garlic until it turns golden. Stir this mixture into the yoghurt sauce.

If you have a microwave, you can lay the pieces of cooked chicken in a serving dish, cover with the sauce and a lid, and reheat for 3–4 minutes on high. Alternatively, lay the pieces of chicken in a wide pan, cover with the sauce and reheat very gently on a hob. Serve with rice and a green salad.

DESSERTS AND BAKING

In Egypt, as all over North Africa, the fresh fruit is so delicious that it forms the basis of most desserts and is often simply eaten by itself at the end of the meal. However, in the days before canning and freezing, the only way to preserve fruits was to dry them – a method ideally suited to a sunny climate. Dried fruits therefore appear in a number of delicious desserts and in the *petits fours* and jams which are often served with coffee after a meal or as a mid-morning snack. Another Egyptian favourite is milk-based ice cream, which is wonderfully refreshing in the heat and tastes not dissimilar to Indian kulfi.

SWEET COUSCOUS WITH DRIED FRUIT SALAD

SERVES 4

115 g/4 oz dried apricots

75 g/3 oz dried figs

1 tsp honey

1 cinnamon stick

4 tbsp couscous

1 tsp caster (superfine) sugar

This sounds like an odd combination but in fact works very well, especially if you have a couscousier and can easily create light and fluffy couscous grains.

Put the apricots and figs in a small pan with the honey and cinnamon and 300 ml/½ pint/1½ cups water. Bring to the boil and simmer for 5–30 minutes, depending on how dry the fruit was. It should end up very soft. Turn into a serving dish or bowl.

Meanwhile, add 3 tbsp boiling water to the couscous and mix it lightly with your fingers. Put the couscous into a couscousier or, if you do not have one, into a heatproof sieve or steamer on top of a deep pan of simmering water. Cover and steam the couscous for 30 minutes or till it is light, soft and fluffy.

When ready to serve, turn the couscous out on to a warmed plate, sprinkle lightly with sugar and serve at once with the warm fruit salad.

KHOSHAF

This macerated fruit salad is not cooked at all, just left for several days to let the water absorb all the subtle flavours of the fruits. Choose your own combinations, and feel free to improvise! Surprisingly, the nuts do not go soggy during their long immersion.

SERVES 6–8

275 g/10 oz mixed dried fruits (dates, prunes, apricots, raisins, figs)

50 g/2 oz nuts (pine nuts, flaked almonds, walnuts, or a mixture)

1 tbsp orange flower water

Put the fruit, nuts and orange flower water into a bowl and just cover with cold water (filtered if possible). Cover the bowl and set aside in a cool larder or on the top shelf of the fridge for at least 36 hours, preferably 48. The fruit will melt into the water, creating a delicious natural syrup. Serve warm or at room temperature with cream or ice cream.

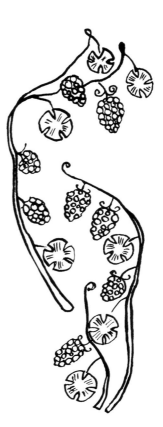

SEMOLINA CAKE

This delicious, rich cake can be served with coffee or as a dessert. The finer the semolina, the more delicate the cake, and because it is soaked in syrup it keeps remarkably well.

SERVES 8–10

115 g/4 oz/½ cup unsalted butter, softened

150 g/6 oz caster (superfine) sugar

2 eggs

50 ml/2 fl oz/½ cup milk

1 tbsp orange flower water

1 tsp vanilla essence

450 g/1 lb semolina

1½ tsp baking powder or soda

25 g/1 oz flaked or sliced almonds

SUGAR SYRUP

125 g/5 oz caster (superfine) sugar

juice of ½ lemon

2 tbsp orange flower water

Beat the butter and sugar together till smooth and light. Add the eggs, one at a time, beating well after each addition. Stir in the milk, orange flower water and vanilla essence, then the semolina and baking powder, making sure that they are very well mixed. Grease a 20 × 20-cm/8 × 8-in baking

tray or dish and pour in the batter. Smooth the top with a spatula and sprinkle on the almonds. Bake in a preheated moderate oven (180°C/350°F/Gas Mark 4) for 25–30 minutes or until firm and lightly browned. Remove from the oven and place on a serving dish.

To make the syrup, put the sugar in a pan with 120 ml/4 fl oz/½ cup water and bring gently to a simmer. Simmer until the sugar is completely dissolved, then remove from the heat. Add the lemon juice and orange flower water and pour the mixture slowly over the cake, allowing the syrup to sink in. Serve at room temperature with a fruit salad or Egyptian ice cream.

HONEY AND CARDAMOM ICE CREAM

This is a delicately flavoured ice cream, ideally served with an equally mild fruit accompaniment. Mastic (a resin from an evergreen shrub, with a liquorice flavour) is quite common in Middle Eastern desserts but is not essential.

475 ml/16 fl oz/2 cups whole milk

1 level tsp arrowroot

150 ml/5 fl oz/⅔ cup double or heavy cream

10 cardamom pods, bruised with a rolling pin

2 tbsp honey

1 tbsp orange flower water

½ tsp crushed mastic (if available)

Mix a little of the milk into the arrowroot to make a smooth cream. Add this to the rest of the milk and the cream. Transfer to a saucepan with the cardamom and honey and bring slowly to the boil. Cook very gently, stirring continuously, until the mixture thickens slightly. Add the orange flower water and crushed mastic (if using) and continue to cook for a few more minutes. Remove from the heat, cover and allow to cool completely. When quite cold, put into an ice-cream maker and churn-freeze till frozen, but not frozen hard. Serve at once if possible. If not, freeze hard, but before serving remove from the freezer and allow to soften in the fridge for at least 30 minutes. Serve with fresh fruit or a macerated fruit salad.

FIG ICE CREAM

You can substitute another dried fruit such as apricots or prunes instead of the figs.

SERVES 6–8

115 g/4 oz dried figs

1 tsp ground cinnamon

475 ml/16 fl oz/2 cups whole milk

475 ml/16 fl oz/2 cups double or heavy cream

1 tbsp dark muscovado sugar

Soften the figs first in boiling water if very hard and chop very small in a food processor. Put the cinnamon in a pan with the milk, cream and dark brown sugar. Bring very slowly to the boil and, as soon as it starts to bubble, remove from the heat. Add the figs, mix well and allow to cool. When quite cold, place in an ice-cream maker and churn-freeze till frozen, but not frozen hard. Serve at once if possible. If not, freeze hard, but before serving remove from the freezer and allow to soften in the fridge for at least 30 minutes. Serve with fresh fruit or a macerated fruit salad.

DRIED FIG AND APRICOT JAM

Around the Middle East, small bowls of exotic jams such as this might be offered to guests to taste with a small silver spoon after a meal or while sipping mid-morning coffee and eating sweet nutty *petits fours* (see pp. 58–9). This jam is also delicious as a spread on bread or warm rolls, a topping for ice cream or stirred into thick creamy yoghurt.

MAKES ABOUT 1 KG/2½ LB

225 g/8 oz dried figs, stems removed

225 g/8 oz dried apricots

225 g/8 oz granulated sugar

juice of ½ lemon

½ tsp aniseed (optional)

2 tbsp pine nuts

50 g/2 oz chopped walnuts

Roughly chop the figs and apricots. Boil the sugar with 300 ml/½ pint/ 1½ cups water and the lemon juice for a minute or two till the sugar is well dissolved. Add the fruit and simmer gently for about 30 minutes or until the fruit is quite soft and the juices have thickened sufficiently to coat the back of a spoon. Stir frequently to make sure it does not stick. Add the aniseed (if using), pine nuts and walnuts and stir thoroughly. Cook for a further few minutes, then pot the jam into warm, sterilized glass jars with tight-fitting lids.

GLAZED WALNUTS

MAKES 15

50 g/2 oz ground almonds

50 g/2 oz caster (superfine) sugar

1–2 tbsp orange flower water

30 walnut halves

50 g/2 oz granulated sugar

Mix the ground almonds with the caster sugar and add sufficient orange flower water to make a thick paste. Sandwich the walnut halves together with the almond paste and lay them on a wire rack placed on a baking tray. Melt the granulated sugar in a heavy saucepan and cook till it is light brown in colour, then carefully pour this over the walnuts so that each is coated. As the caramel cools it will hold the walnut halves together.

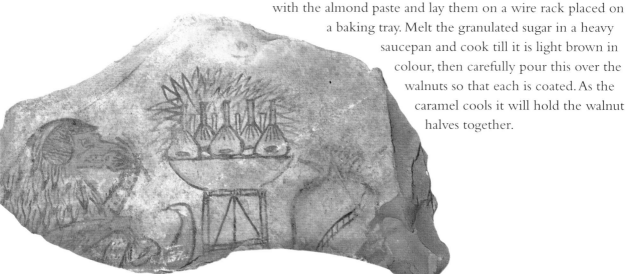

MA'MOUL

MAKES 36 LITTLE PASTRIES

250 g/9 oz butter

500 g/1½ lb plain flour

2 tbsp orange flower water

3 tbsp milk

FILLING

175 g/6 oz broken walnut pieces

125 g/5 oz dried figs, softened in boiling water if very hard

2 tbsp orange flower water

1 tsp ground cinnamon

2 tbsp caster (superfine) sugar

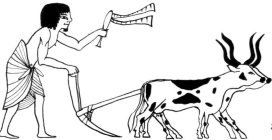

Rub the butter into the flour till it is crumbly, then work in the orange flower water and milk until you have a soft pastry dough.

To make the filling, chop the walnuts and figs very finely either by hand or in a food processor. Add the orange flower water, cinnamon and sugar and mix well.

Break off a piece of dough the size of a golf ball and flatten it into a circle in the palm of your hand. Place a tbsp of the filling in the middle of the dough and encase the filling by bringing the outside edges of the circle in towards the middle and pressing the edges together. Repeat the process until all the dough and filling are used up. Place the pastries, spaced fairly well apart, on an ungreased baking tray and bake in a preheated moderate oven (180°C/350°F/Gas Mark 4) for 20–25 minutes or until lightly tanned and crisp. Remove from the oven and allow to cool.

Alternatively, roll the dough out into a large rectangle and cut it into strips about 5 cm/2 in wide. With a palette knife, spread the filling over the dough strips, then roll them up lengthways. With a very sharp knife, cut the rolls into slices or 'pinwheels' about 1 cm/½ in thick. Bake as above but for 10–15 minutes.

BREADS

Bread is the most ancient of Egyptian foods and there is anthropological evidence to suggest that it was baked from the earliest times. Early breads were made from barley and millet, and from wheat which had been heated in order to remove its husk. Barley and millet are low in gluten, while heating wheat reduced its gluten content – which meant that early breads were quite hard and chewy. The development of a wheat which could be threshed without heating and thereby retain its gluten was the first move towards lighter modern bread. Flour made from ancient forms of wheat such as spelt (obtainable from healthfood stores) comes close to that of the early Egyptians.

Today Egyptian bread is nearly always flat but sufficiently leavened to puff up and form a pocket, which can be used for scooping other foods. It is soft and quickly goes stale but freezes well and then can easily be refreshed by damping and reheating. Alternatively it can be stored in a closed plastic bag or on a dish tightly covered with cling film to prevent it drying out. It is usually made from a combination of white and wholemeal flours, but can be all brown (as in the spelt recipe opposite) or all white for 'fine dining'.

EGYPTIAN FLAT BREAD

MAKES ABOUT 8 PITTA

500 g/1½ lb spelt or other strong bread flour (brown or white)

½ tsp salt

7-g/⅓-oz sachet easy-blend dried yeast

300 ml/½ pint/1½ cups tepid water (one-third boiling to two-thirds cold)

Mix the flour with the salt and yeast in a large bowl. Make a well in the centre and pour in the water. Gradually draw the flour into the water and mix to a soft dough. Knead by hand on a floured board for 15 minutes, or for 10 minutes in a food processor fitted with a dough hook. Pour a little oil into the bottom of a bowl, roll the dough in it and cover the bowl with a clean damp cloth or cling film. Put in a warm place for 1½–2 hours or until the dough has almost doubled in size.

Remove the dough from the bowl and 'knock back' or punch it down. Knead it again for another 3–4 minutes, then cut into eight pieces. On a floured board, flatten out each piece into a round (about 5 mm/½ inch thick) with your hand or a rolling pin. Sprinkle with cold water to prevent browning. Transfer to a floured baking tray and bake in a preheated hot oven (220°C/425°F/Gas Mark 7) for 8–10 minutes. Do not open the oven door while the bread is baking. Each bread should puff up, leaving a pocket in the middle. Remove from the oven and cool slightly on a wire rack.

SESAME RINGS

MAKES 2 RINGS

500 g/1½ lb strong white bread flour

½ tsp salt

1 tsp sugar

7-g/⅓-oz sachet easy-blend dried yeast

300 ml/½ pint/1½ cups tepid water
(one-third boiling to two-thirds cold)

2 tbsp olive oil

1 egg

sesame seeds for sprinkling

Mix the flour, salt, sugar and yeast in a large bowl and make a well in the centre. Pour in the water and oil and gradually draw in the flour. Knead on a floured board for 15 minutes, or for 10 minutes in a food processor fitted with a dough hook. Pour a little oil into a bowl, roll the dough in it and cover the bowl with a clean damp cloth or cling film. Put in a warm place for 1½–2 hours or until the dough has almost doubled in size.

Take the dough out of the bowl, 'knock back' or punch it down and knead again for a further 5 minutes. Cut the dough in half and roll each half into a sausage shape that you can form into a ring with a diameter of about 20 cm/8 in, about 5 cm/2 in thick. Lay the rings on an oiled baking tray. Beat the egg with 2 tbsp water and glaze the tops of the rings. Sprinkle generously with sesame seeds and bake in a preheated hot oven (220°C/425°F/Gas Mark 7) for 10 minutes, then reduce the heat to 150°C/300°F/Gas Mark 2 for a further 15 minutes. Remove from the oven and cool on a wire rack.

FURTHER READING

A New Book of Middle Eastern Food by
Claudia Roden, Viking, London, 1985.
A delightful book, both informed and
informative, and a delicious introduction
by a world-famous expert on Middle
Eastern food.

Middle Eastern Cookery by Suzy Benghiat,
Weidenfeld & Nicholson, London, 1984.
Another excellent introduction to Middle
Eastern food. The author was brought up
in Egypt.

The Complete Middle East Cookbook by Tess
Mallos, Lansdowne Press, Sydney, 1979.
Fascinating recipes and introductions to the
food of countries bordering the eastern
Mediterranean.

An Ancient Egyptian Herbal by Lise Manniche,
British Museum Press, London, 2006.

The British Museum Book of Ancient Egypt
edited by A. J. Spencer, British Museum Press,
London, 2007.

The British Museum Dictionary of Ancient Egypt
by Ian Shaw and Paul Nicholson,
British Museum Press, London, 2008.

Women in Ancient Egypt by Gay Robins,
British Museum Press, London, 2004.

Write Your Own Egyptian Hieroglyphs
by Angela McDonald, British Museum Press,
London, 2007.

INDEX OF RECIPES

ILLUSTRATIONS